polar animals

By Susan Hayes and
Tory Gordon-Harris

Free digital book

Read the incredible, adventurous, and daring tales of polar explorers in your free digital book.

amazing polar explorers

A digital companion to **Polar Animals**

SCHOLASTIC

Download your all-new digital book,

Amazing Polar Explorers

Log on to
www.scholastic.com/discovermore

Enter this special code:

RCC6XWGJR2WG

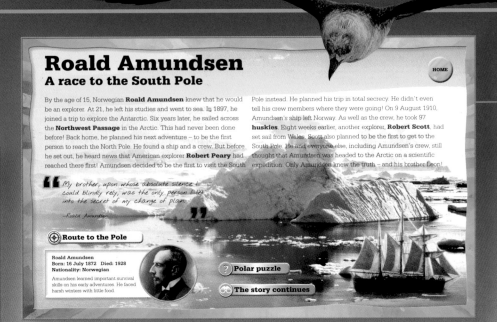

Roald Amundsen
A race to the South Pole

By the age of 15, Norwegian **Roald Amundsen** knew that he would be an explorer. At 21, he left his studies and went to sea. In 1897, he joined a trip to explore the Antarctic. Six years later, he sailed across the **Northwest Passage** in the Arctic. This had never been done before! Back home, he planned his next adventure – to be the first person to reach the North Pole. He found a ship and a crew. But before he set out, he heard news that American explorer **Robert Peary** had reached there first! Amundsen decided to be the first to visit the South

Pole instead. He planned his trip in total secrecy. He didn't even tell his crew members where they were going! On 9 August 1910, Amundsen's ship left Norway. As well as the crew, he took 97 **huskies**. Eight weeks earlier, another explorer, **Robert Scott**, had set sail from Wales. Scott also planned to be the first to get to the South Pole. He and everyone else, including Amundsen's crew, still thought that Amundsen was headed to the Arctic on a scientific expedition. Only Amundsen knew the truth – and his brother Leon!

> *My brother, upon whose absolute silence I could blindly rely, was the only person I let into the secret of my change of plan.*
> –Roald Amundsen

Route to the Pole

Roald Amundsen
Born: 16 July 1872   Died: 1928
Nationality: Norwegian
Amundsen learned important survival skills on his early adventures. He faced harsh winters with little food.

? Polar puzzle

The story continues

Meet the explorer who reached the South Pole before anyone else, ever.

husky

Huskies are large dogs that originally came from the Arctic parts of Greenland, Canada, Alaska, and northern Siberia (in Russia). Greenland dogs and Siberian huskies are two breeds, or types, of husky. Roald Amundsen took Greenland dogs to the South Pole to pull sleds full of equipment and food on his expedition. Huskies are still used to pull sleds and for sled racing in icy conditions.

Huskies are among the oldest types of dog in the world. They are pack dogs and like to be with other dogs.

A husky's toes are spaced close together, and its feet are tough.

Huskies are used to snow and icy weather. They have very thick coats that are usually white or grey, but they can also be black or even red.

There are infopops and fun quizzes for you to enjoy.

Fit for the frost?

Would you survive a polar expedition? Think about what you would need for your trip. Now click on the items that you would **not** bring!

Now join the hunt. Can you find ten objects that you would take to the poles?

You will hear a fanfare if you choose the right objects!

It's simple to get your digital book. Go to the website (see left), enter the code, and download the book. Make sure you open it using Adobe Reader.

GO!

Consultant:
Kim Dennis-Bryan, PhD

Copyright © 2014 by Scholastic Inc.

All rights reserved. Published by Scholastic Inc.,
Publishers since 1920. SCHOLASTIC, SCHOLASTIC
DISCOVER MORE™, and associated logos are trademarks and/
or registered trademarks of Scholastic Inc.

Distributed in the UK by
Scholastic UK Ltd
Westfield Road
Southam, Warwickshire
England CV47 0RA

Library of Congress Cataloging-in-Publication
Data Available

ISBN 978 1407 14249 4

10 9 8 7 6 5 4 3 2 1   14 15 16 17 18

Printed in Singapore   46
First published 2014

Scholastic is constantly working to lessen the
environmental impact of our manufacturing
processes. To view our industry-leading
paper procurement policy, visit
www.scholastic.com/paperpolicy.

Contents

The ends of the Earth

The Arctic

The ends of the Earth

Welcome to the top and the bottom of the world. The Arctic Circle surrounds the North Pole. Antarctica surrounds the South Pole. In these huge, wild places, land and sea are frozen for much of the year. The snow sparkles, the sea ice dazzles, and glaciers tower into vast skies.

Polar animals

More than 99 per cent of all the ice on Earth's surface is at the poles! Polar animals have cool ways of keeping warm. They may be very fat, or furry, or covered in dense feathers.

bearded seal

least weasel

reindeer

Arctic hare

ermine

black guillemot

emperor penguin

harp seal pup

Atlantic puffin

Arctic fox

wandering albatross

wolverine

cape petrel

snow petrel

polar bear

south polar skua

imperial shag

Canadian lynx kitten

Adélie penguin

snowy owl

chinstrap penguin

Arctic lemming

little auk

king penguin chick

musk ox

leopard seal

musk ox calf

Life in the big chill

Arctic temperatures can drop to −40°C (−40°F) in the dark, stormy winter. Even in the Antarctic summer, it stays close to freezing, at just over 0°C (32°F). No trees grow. Food is hard to find. Polar animals are built to survive some of the harshest conditions on Earth.

How cold?

The coldest temperature ever recorded was at the South Pole, in Antarctica. It was off the scale at −94.7°C (−138.5°F)!

Warm fur

A thick coat of fur traps warm air to keep a polar bear cub's body warm.

Fighting ice and cold

Blubber

A thick layer of blubber, or body fat, acts like a blanket to keep a sea mammal warm.

Snowshoes

Large feet keep some animals from sinking into the snow. Furry toes grip the ground.

Super senses

Incredible eyesight, sense of smell, and hearing help many polar animals hunt their prey in the snow.

about penguins on
pages 54–57.

Find out more
about penguins on
pages 54–57.

Packed feathers

A penguin has lots of
short feathers packed
closely together. Along
with a layer of fat, they
keep out the cold.

*A plump layer of
fat helps to keep
a penguin warm.*

Antifreeze

Some fish have a special
protein in their bodies. It acts
like antifreeze to cope with
the coldest waters on Earth.

Adélie ......
penguin

Polar babies

Life on the ice is hard when you're a baby! Not only is it extremely cold, but there aren't many places to hide from predators. And your parents might need to travel a very long way to find food for you.

Camouflage
A harp seal pup's white coat helps it hide from hungry polar bears. Its adult coat will be grey.

Living alone
A polar bear cub usually stays with its mother for two to two and a half years, until it can survive on its own.

Keeping warm

Thousands of emperor penguin chicks huddle together in a group called a crèche, to keep warm in the biting cold.

Protected by the herd

A musk ox calf is a tasty meal for an Arctic wolf. When under attack, adult musk oxen will form a circle around the young to protect them.

Waiting for dinner

Wandering albatross parents travel incredible distances – up to 15,000 kilometres (9,300 miles) – to bring food back to their young.

A wandering albatross chick takes food from its mother's beak.

Ice baby

A Weddell seal is born on the Antarctic ice. It fattens up quickly on its mother's milk and develops a thick layer of blubber, or fat, to keep warm.

Long sleep

Weddells rest and sleep on the ice for hours at a time. As they bask in the sunshine, their body heat melts hollows in the ice beneath them.

Cold poles

Both the Arctic (the North Pole) and the Antarctic (the South Pole) are cold because they don't get much direct sunlight. At both poles, summer is sunnier than winter is.

North Pole

axis .....

The Earth travels around the Sun. Its axis is tilted. When the South Pole is tilted towards the Sun, it is summer there. But it is winter at the North Pole.

South Pole

Reflection

White ice reflects the Sun's rays like a mirror. Most of the heat bounces back into space. That's another reason why it's cold at the poles.

When it is light and summer at the South Pole, it is dark and winter at the North Pole, and vice versa.

The North and South Poles are each in darkness for

Arctic tern

The North Pole is in the Arctic.

The Arctic

Most of the Arctic is a frozen ocean with no land underneath it. But in the winter, Arctic snow and ice extend to the tips of three different continents: North America, Europe, and Asia.

Arctic Circle

Asia

polar bear

Europe

North America

Arctic fox

Polar bears live on the ice and snow in the Arctic.

Africa

Arctic tern

The Antarctic

Antarctica is a continent, or large land mass, surrounded by the Southern Ocean. It is covered by a thick sheet of ice.

South America

Antarctic Circle

The South Pole is in the Antarctic.

gentoo penguins

chinstrap penguin

Southern Ocean

Australia

Penguins live in the Antarctic. Polar bears and penguins never meet!

six months, or half the year.

Arctic seasons

In the winter, the Arctic is dark and locked in ice. Many animals leave. In the spring, much of this frozen world melts away in the sunlight. The animals come back and feast all summer on the tundra.

**SPRING
March – May**

glaucous gull ......

The Sun peeps over the horizon and the melt begins. Polar bear cubs come out of their dens, and seal pups are born.

.... polar bear cub

**SUMMER
June – August**

The Sun never sets. Babies are born, and visiting birds and animals have plenty to eat.

.... glaucous gull chick

Arctic fox kit ....

Summer feasting

In the summer, food is plentiful on the Arctic tundra, where the ice has vanished. There are no trees, but grass grows and flowers bloom. Animals can eat day and night.

The Arctic is called the Land of the Midnight Sun,

The melt

In the summer, the sea ice melts under the Sun's rays. It crackles and breaks into great chunks and slowly melts into the Arctic Ocean.

summer

winter

KEY

sea ice

Summer versus winter

By the end of the Arctic summer, an area of ice the size of Australia will have melted.

AUTUMN
September – October

The days get shorter. Many animals leave for warmer lands and seas.

······humpback whale

WINTER
November – February

Only a few animals stay for the dark, freezing winter.

······bearded seal

Bleak winter

Only the toughest animals survive the Arctic winter. Musk oxen use their sharp hooves to dig through the snow. They find moss, lichen, and roots to eat.

 Find out more about musk oxen on pages 46–47.

musk·· ox

because there is no night-time at all during the summer.

Antarctic seasons

When it is summer in the Arctic, it is winter in the Antarctic. Winter is even colder at the bottom of the world. But when spring comes, the frozen ocean surrounding Antarctica melts almost completely.

Adélie penguins ·······

ANTARCTIC SEASONS

SPRING
September – November

The days get longer, and the great melt begins. Animals arrive to nest and breed.

·· Adélie penguins

SUMMER
December – February

The Sun never sets. Babies are born. Food is plentiful.

Weddell seal cub ······

The richest ocean on Earth

As the sea ice melts in the spring, thousands of whales arrive. Some eat up to 4 tonnes of krill a day.

There are 100–500 million tons of shrimp-like krill in Antarctica's Southern Ocean.

The weight of all the krill in the Southern Ocean equals

Summer visitors

Adélie penguins spend all winter at sea. In the spring, they come back to Antarctica to breed.

summer   **winter**

Summer versus winter

In the summer, Antarctica is almost one and a half times the size of the United States. In the winter, it doubles in size.

AUTUMN
March – May

The days get shorter. Most animals leave. The wandering albatross stays to raise its chick.

WINTER
June – August

The Antarctic winter is brutal. The male emperor penguin is the only warm-blooded animal that stays.

Tough winter residents

Male emperor penguins protect one another from Antarctica's extreme winter weather by clumping together in a huddle.

 Find out more
about emperors on pages 54–57.

that of all the people on Earth.

Hall of fame

In extreme places, animals may also be extreme! Meet some of the record-breakers of the Arctic and the Antarctic. Many of them hold world records, too!

LONGEST POLAR TOOTH
The narwhal's tusk is actually a very long tooth. It can grow up to 2.7 m (9 ft). That's as long as a one-storey building is tall.

WORLD'S LONGEST MAMMAL MIGRATION
The humpback whale travels further than any other mammal – 16,400 km (10,200 miles) a year.

WORLD'S HEAVIEST SEABIRD CHICK
A wandering albatross chick can reach 10 kg (22 lbs) in weight – as much as an adult swan.

WORLD'S HEAVIEST SEAL
Antarctica's southern elephant seal can weigh as much as 4,000 kg (8,800 lbs).

WORLD'S LARGEST LAND PREDATOR

The heaviest recorded male polar bear weighed 1,000 kg (2,210 lbs). Polar bears are powerful and very dangerous, even to humans.

WORLD'S LONGEST-LIVING CATERPILLAR

The Arctic woolly bear moth is a caterpillar for seven years before it turns into a moth.

WORLD'S FASTEST BIRD

The peregrine falcon dives from the sky at 320 kph (200 mph).

WORLD'S LONGEST BIRD MIGRATION

The Arctic tern travels 80,000 km (50,000 miles) every year, from the Arctic to the Antarctic and back again.

WORLD'S BIGGEST LIVING ANIMAL

The blue whale is the heaviest animal in the world today. The heaviest recorded was 172 tonnes.

LARGEST LAND ANIMAL IN ANTARCTICA

The largest animal on land in Antarctica all year long is the Antarctic midge.

The Arctic

The word *Arctic* comes from the ancient Greek word for "bear". The polar bear, one of Earth's most ferocious predators, lives on this frozen ocean.

Ice bear

Alone, the 725-kilogram (1,600-lbs) polar bear prowls the Arctic ice. It is looking for seals – its favourite food. Caught between teeth like daggers, a seal won't stand a chance.

Storing fat

Polar bears like blubbery seals. The bears store fat in their bodies to live off when food is scarce.

Seal hunt

Sense of smell

A polar bear can smell prey up to 32 kilometres (20 miles) away, and 1 m (3 ft) under snow.

Watch and wait

The bear waits patiently next to a seal's breathing hole, sometimes for days at a time.

The end

When the seal finally surfaces, the bear gets down on all fours and catches it in its jaws.

The biggest polar bears can eat 68 kilograms (150 lbs) of

When the sea ice melts in the summer, it is more difficult for polar bears to hunt seals. They will eat anything they can find, even attacking sharp-tusked walruses!

CATCH OF THE DAY

narwhal

harp seal pup

tern eggs

kelp

walrus

ringed seal

rubbish

harp seal ....
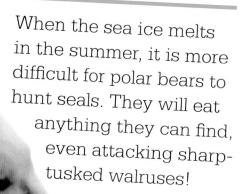

Lucky escape

A seal usually keeps 10 to 15 breathing holes open. It surfaces every 20 minutes. A polar bear can only wait by one hole at a time, so the seal can often escape.

blubber in just one meal!

Bringing up baby

During the Arctic winter, a polar bear mother may give birth to one, two, or three cubs. She feeds them in a warm den under the snow until spring.

Beneath the snow

In the autumn, a pregnant bear digs a tunnel into the snow to make a den for herself and her cubs.

A polar bear's skin is black underneath its fur. Dark

See me grow A polar bear cub's first year

1 Newborn

Polar bear cubs are born with downy fur and no teeth. They are blind, too. The cubs drink milk from their mother and grow quickly.

2 Leaving the den

The mother digs her way out of the den in the spring. Her cubs follow her. They have never been outside before.

3 Finding food

The mother hunts for food. She will eat almost anything she can find! In deep snow or water, she may carry her cubs on her back.

4 Learning to hunt

The cubs stay with their mother until they have learned to hunt on their own.

skin soaks up the Sun's warming rays.

Sea bear

Polar bears are incredible swimmers. They can swim for days without stopping and have been spotted 100 kilometres (60 miles) from shore. Their large, flat front paws are used as paddles in the water. Their back paws act as a rudder, for steering.

Drying off
After a swim, a polar bear shakes off as much water as possible from its fur. It then rubs itself against the snow to dry off.

Seals and walruses

Thick layers of blubber keep seals and walruses warm in the icy Arctic water. Although rather slow on land, they are speedy and streamlined in water.

Ice seals

bearded seal

On the ice

Seal pups are born on the ice. They eat and sleep there for a few weeks. Newborn harp seal pups have yellow coats. They become white after about three days.

When this harp seal pup sheds its baby fur, there will be a spotted, waterproof coat underneath.

Watchful mother

A newborn pup feeds from its mother's milk. The mother can recognize her pup from hundreds of others by its smell.

All alone

At 12 days old, the pup has built up enough blubber to survive on its own. Its mother leaves. At 4 weeks, the pup will swim and fish for itself.

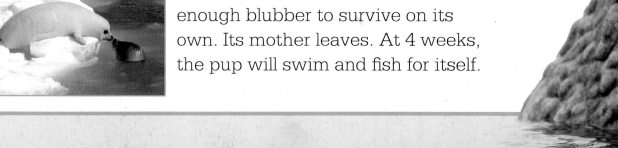

There are six different types of seal in the Arctic.

ringed seal

spotted seal

hooded seal

ribbon seal

harp seal

Swim for supper

Adult seals are great divers. Some can reach depths of 400 metres (1,300 ft). Big eyes, sensitive whiskers, and good hearing help them find their prey in dark, murky waters.

Arctic seals eat lots of different types of food, including small fish and shellfish.

.clams

Walruses use their whiskers as feelers to find shellfish near the seafloor.

The mighty walrus

The hefty walrus hauls itself out of the water with its tusks. At up to 1.45 tonnes in weight, it moves clumsily on land. But in water it can swim steadily and non-stop for over 160 kilometres (100 miles).

Walrus beach

In the sea, a walrus's skin is white. In sunlight, blood

Big squeeze
Walruses spend
two-thirds of their lives
at sea. For a few weeks
each year, they gather on
beaches in huge numbers.
Up to 14,000 may cram
themselves onto a
single beach.

flows to the skin's surface, and the walrus changes colour.

White whales

Narwhals and belugas belong to the white whale family. Their colour camouflages them in the Arctic ice, hiding them from polar bears and orcas. Beneath the ice, these whales catch fish and squid using echolocation.

Narwhals The unicorns of the north

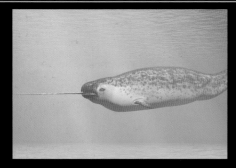

Tusks

No one is sure why a narwhal has a tusk. Occasionally, males have two. Tusks can grow to 2.7 metres (9 ft)!

Friendly groups

Narwhals gather in large groups. Scientists think they may use echolocation to "talk" as well as to hunt.

A narwhal's swordlike tusk is actually a hollow tooth. It keeps growing throughout the narwhal's life.

Belugas are also called sea canaries, because of the

Winter ice hole

In winter, a beluga must keep an ice hole open so that it can surface, or come up, to breathe.

Summer migration

In summer, thousands of belugas migrate to warm, shallow waters further south.

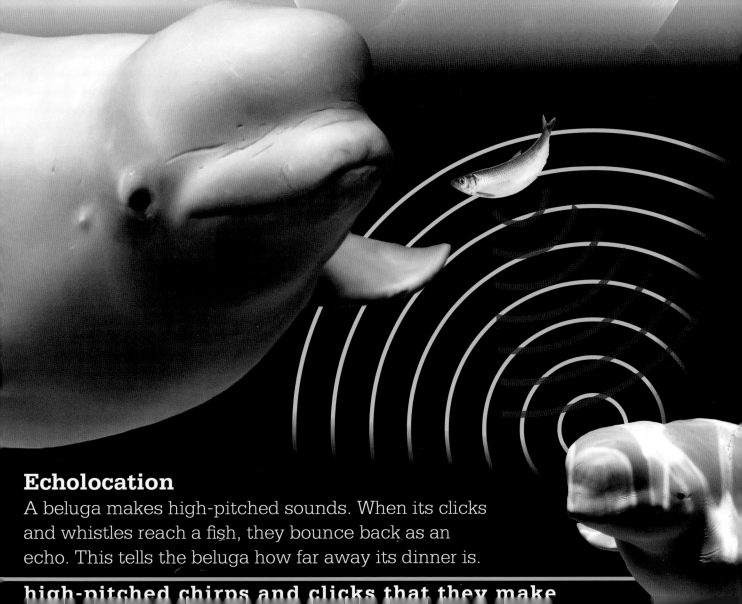

Echolocation

A beluga makes high-pitched sounds. When its clicks and whistles reach a fish, they bounce back as an echo. This tells the beluga how far away its dinner is.

high-pitched chirps and clicks that they make

Arctic ghost

The snowy owl is as silent as a ghost as it glides down to catch its prey. It will hunt from dawn to dusk to feed itself and its chicks.

Powerful hunter

The snowy owl is a big bird of prey, up to 71 cm (28 ins) tall. Its keen eyes and ears help it find food. Its sharp beak and talons dig into prey.

Perfect dinner

A lemming, which is about the size of a mouse, is a snowy owl's favourite food.

A snowy owl will eat 3 to 5 lemmings a day – that's as

Owlets See a baby snowy owl grow.

1 Clutch of eggs

The female snowy owl builds her nest on the ground. She lays between 3 and 11 eggs. The eggs hatch after 4 to 5 weeks.

2 Young chicks

Baby owls are covered in fluffy white down. They cheep, hiss, and squeal while their parents hunt silently and bring food back to the nest.

An older owlet's soft down is dark brown. As the owlet grows, light-coloured feathers replace the dark down.

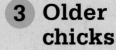

3 Older chicks

The owlets quickly grow into football-sized balls of fluff. Their parents feed them until they fledge, or fly away, and can hunt for themselves.

many as 1,825 a year!

Arctic hare

A wolf is on the prowl, and the Arctic hare must hide. Its clever coat is perfect camouflage, whether it is summer or winter.

Summer coat

In the summer, the hare is camouflaged in the rocks and grasses of the tundra by its short grey-brown coat.

Arctic hares have black eyelashes that protect their

Winter coat

In the winter, the hare's super thick white coat camouflages it in the snow and also keeps it warm.

eyes from the Sun's glare, just like sunglasses do.

Chasing the Sun

The Arctic has many summer visitors. Animals migrate, or travel, there from all over the world. Food is plentiful in the seas and on the tundra.

Following the Sun

The Arctic tern flies all the way from the Arctic to the Antarctic and back again – every year! It chases warm skies and summer sunlight all year long.

Arctic terns usually feed as they fly.

Return to nest

Imagine watching 5 million snow geese fly overhead! They travel in huge flocks from Mexico to the Arctic tundra to breed in the springtime.

Thick down feathers help keep the geese warm as they fly.

Long-distance lunch

In the summer, the Arctic seas teem with life. To grey and northern humpback whales, these seas are a huge, delicious soup. They travel there to feed every year.

Grey whales feast on small sea animals all summer.

42

The Arctic tern sees two summers each year, and more

The Arctic tern travels
2 million km
(1.25 million miles) in a lifetime
(that's the same as going **to the Moon and back** three times!)

Arctic

Antarctic

The tern flies 40,000 km (25,000 miles) each way.

Chicks are raised on the Arctic tundra.

Watch out, geese! The Arctic fox is on the lookout for a tasty meal.

Find out more about humpback whales on pages 59–61.

When summer draws to an end, northern humpback whales return south to warmer waters. Their journey takes two to three months.

daylight than any other creature on the planet.

Arctic visitors

Millions of birds fly to the tundra in the summer. Snow geese glide in from the east coast of the USA; skuas fly from Australia. The fast, tough peregrine falcon arrives from Central America.

cliff swallows

stonechat

Swainson's thrush

sandhill crane

pomarine skua

American pipit

glaucous-winged gull

whinchat

greater white-fronted geese

Arctic skuas

Arctic tern

semipalmated sandpiper

Eurasian golden plover

ruddy turnstone

snow goose

red-throated diver

red-necked phalarope

black-throated diver

peregrine falcon

long-tailed skua

tundra swans

long-tailed skua

rough-legged buzzard

northern wheatear

white-crowned sparrow

brambling

Lapland bunting

horned lark

common redpoll

bluethroat

Baird's sandpiper

semipalmated plover

American tree sparrow

white-tailed eagle

meadow pipit

spotted sandpiper

upland sandpiper

northern pintail

sanderling

red-breasted merganser

fox sparrow

long-tailed duck

greater scaup

green-winged teal

45

Wolf v. musk ox

A male musk ox is almost ten times the weight of an Arctic wolf. But when food is scarce, a hungry wolf pack will still hunt this dangerous prey.

ARCTIC WOLF	
DIET	musk oxen, reindeer, hares, ptarmigans
AVERAGE HEIGHT	0.9 metres (3 ft)
WEIGHT	25–40 kilograms (55–88 lbs)
SPEED	Up to 56 kph (35 mph)
GROUPS	2–20 wolves in a pack
SPECIAL FEATURES	Has superb hearing and sense of smell for tracking prey. Has strong jaws and sharp teeth for tearing flesh.

A double coat of fur keeps the wolf warm.

The hunt

1 Tracking

A wolf pack follows the scent of a herd of oxen. When the wolves reach the herd, they need to isolate a young or weak ox.

Wolves have incredibly sensitive ears and can track

MUSK OX

DIET
moss, lichen, roots

AVERAGE HEIGHT
1.2–1.5 metres (4–5 ft)

WEIGHT
200–410 kilograms
(440–900 lbs)

SPEED
Up to 60 kph (37 mph)

GROUPS
5–12 in summer herd;
12–30 in winter herd

SPECIAL FEATURES
Uses horns as weapons.
Has horny boss that
protects skull. Can
charge at predators.
Has feet that grip ice.

A horny boss protects the ox during fights.

2 The kill
The oxen form a ring around their young. The wolves work together to separate a weak ox. They then move in for the kill.

The ox's shaggy fur keeps it warm.

Short, very strong legs support its massive body.

Reindeer journey

Every year, thousands of reindeer travel over 5,000 km (3,100 miles) across the Arctic tundra.

spring

Spring

In March, female reindeer leave their winter feeding grounds. The males follow a few weeks later. Massive herds trek through snow and ice for more than ten weeks.

golden eagle

early summer

Early summer

Calves are born in June. They are easy prey for hungry wolves and sharp-eyed eagles, so they stay close to the herd.

Arctic wolf

Midsummer

After just a few weeks, it is time to move on again. The reindeer travel over vast plains and rivers to their summer feeding-grounds.

midsummer

A newborn calf can stand and walk in just a

Winter

When the first snow starts to fall, the reindeer move south to warmer lands. As they travel, they grow thicker, greyer coats to keep them warm in winter.

autumn

Autumn

The reindeer fatten up for the winter with berries, fungi, lichen, and grass. They shed the velvet from their antlers.

Late summer

Summer food is plentiful, but so are mosquitoes and blackflies. The reindeer graze on windy hills to try to avoid these pests.

.....mosquitoes

late summer

few hours.

49

Living in harmony

For thousands of years, Inuit peoples have lived in the Arctic Circle. Conditions are tough, and their survival depends on the animals that live there.

Reindeer people

Some Inuit peoples herd reindeer. They do not live in one place. They follow the reindeer as they migrate through the seasons (see pages 48–49).

......reindeer

A herder's life

Reindeer skins

Herders use reindeer skins to make tents, tools, and clothes. They also eat reindeer meat.

Huskies

Teams of husky dogs pull the herders' sleds across the snow. Huskies are strong, smart, and hardy.

Some Arctic peoples used to sleep with their huskies at

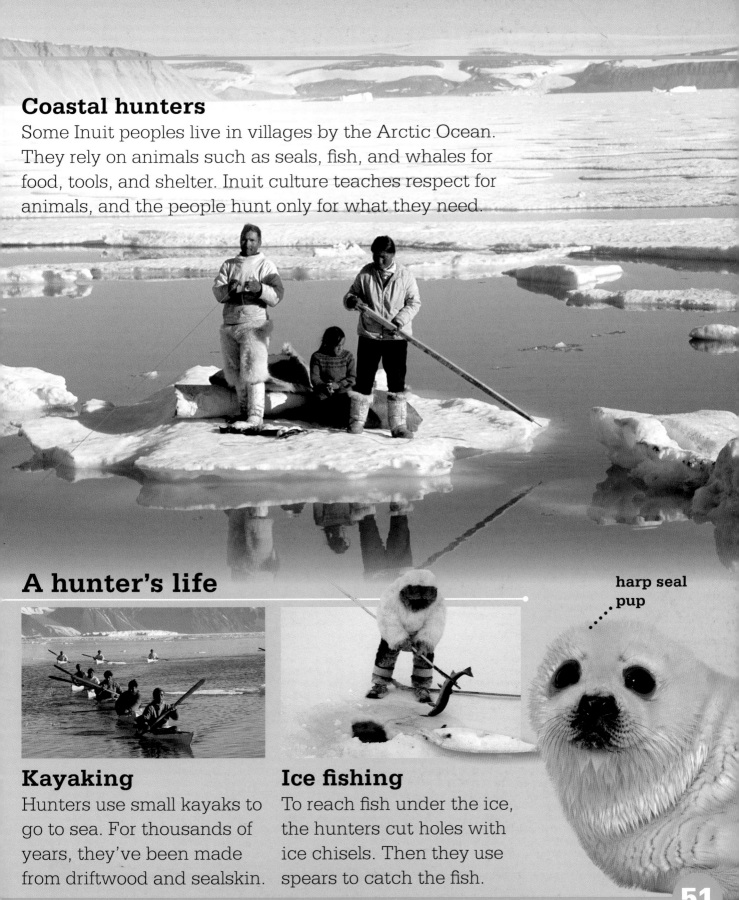

Coastal hunters

Some Inuit peoples live in villages by the Arctic Ocean. They rely on animals such as seals, fish, and whales for food, tools, and shelter. Inuit culture teaches respect for animals, and the people hunt only for what they need.

A hunter's life

harp seal pup

Kayaking

Hunters use small kayaks to go to sea. For thousands of years, they've been made from driftwood and sealskin.

Ice fishing

To reach fish under the ice, the hunters cut holes with ice chisels. Then they use spears to catch the fish.

night to keep warm. It was like having a furry blanket.

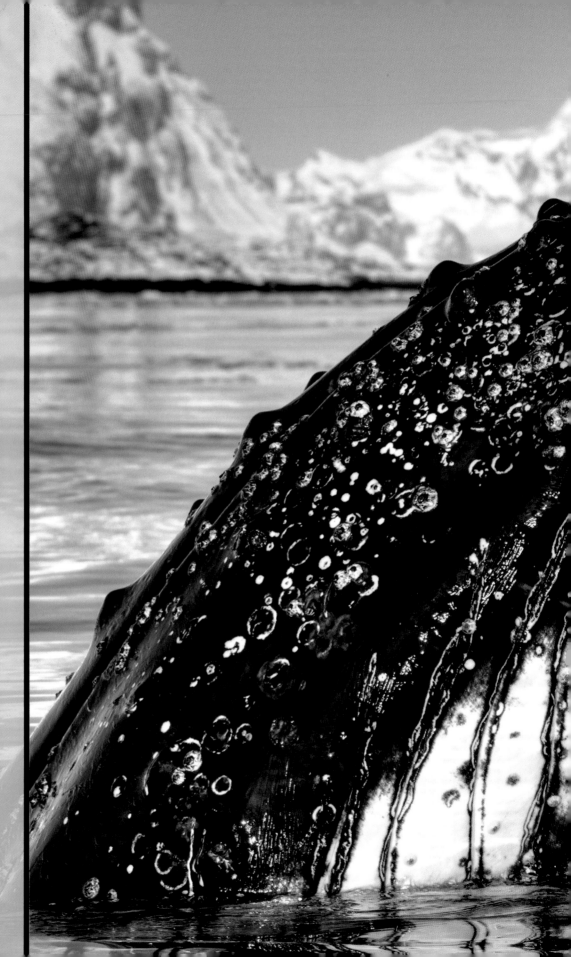

The Antarctic

Icy Antarctica sprawls across the bottom of the world. In the summer, its seas teem with food for seals, penguins, and gigantic, barnacle-covered whales, like this humpback.

March of the penguins

As winter approaches, emperor penguins march non-stop, day and night, up to 110 kilometres (70 miles) across the snow and ice to breed.

Incredible journey

At the end of their long trip, the penguins find their mates. Each couple produces one precious egg.

Precious egg   The female lays her egg,

1 Egg

At the beginning of the Antarctic winter, the female penguin lays a single pear-shaped egg.

2 Pass the egg

She carefully passes the fragile egg to the father's feet. It must not drop onto the ice, or it could freeze.

Emperors are the only penguins that

Find out more about emperor penguins on the next page.

Tobogganing can take the weight off a penguin's tired feet.

Courtship

A male and a female call and bow to impress each other.

then returns to the sea.

Huddling heroes

The penguin dads keep the eggs warm throughout the bitter winter. Hundreds of them huddle together for warmth.

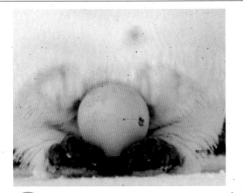

3 Foot rest

The father balances the egg on his feet. He then covers it with his brood pouch (a warm fold of skin).

spend the winter on Antarctica.

Watch me grow

An emperor penguin chick hatches at the end of the Antarctic winter. Its father kept the egg safe for over two months. He has not eaten at all. Now he must care for the new chick until its mother returns.

Soft down

An emperor chick is covered in a layer of woolly down. When it is older, it will moult. A coat of shiny, waterproof feathers will replace the soft down.

AUGUST

Hatchling

A new chick snuggles between its father's legs for warmth.

Finding the chick

An emperor penguin can recognize its own chick's special whistle in a crowd.

SEPTEMBER – OCTOBER

Mother returns

After two months at sea, the mother returns with squid and fish.

OCTOBER – NOVEMBER

Crèche

Both parents go fishing when the chick is old enough to wait in a crèche with other chicks.

DECEMBER

Moulting

When its feathers have moulted, the chick goes to sea and fishes for itself.

Ocean giants

Whales are incredibly big. They are also graceful and smart. They sing songs to one another that can be heard for long distances across the polar oceans.

Deep divers

A whale holds its breath as it dives into the murky waters beneath the ocean waves. Sperm whales can reach depths of more than 1,000 metres (3,300 ft)!

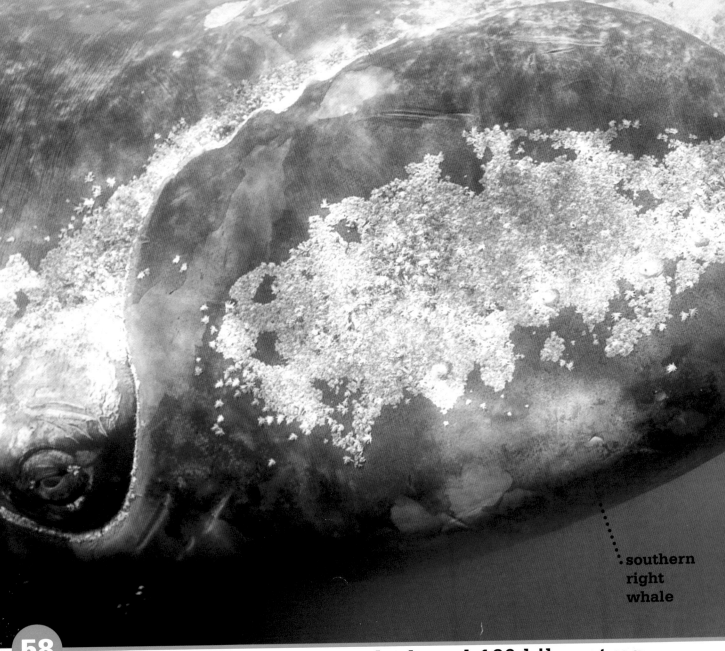

southern right whale

The blue whale's song can be heard 160 kilometres

Krill feast Whales migrate to Antarctica to feed.

A whale can carry up to half a tonne of barnacles on its skin.

Plentiful krill

As spring arrives in Antarctica, thousands of whales do, too. Many of them come to eat the billions of krill in the Southern Ocean.

Bubble nets

Humpback whales work together to catch krill. They make circles of bubbles on the water's surface, which act like big fishing nets.

baleen ...

Huge sieves

Krill-eating whales have plates inside their mouths that look like brushes. Called baleen, they act like giant sieves that trap krill.

The blue whale is the largest living animal.

blue whale
24–27 m (78–88 ft)

southern right whale
14–17 m (45–55 ft)

humpback whale
15–19 m (48–62 ft)

minke whale
11 m (35 ft)

human
1.7 m (5.5 ft)

(100 miles) away. It's as loud as a jet engine!

Water acrobatics

The mighty humpback whale can jump right out of the water and even turn in mid-air. As it crashes back into the waves, its splash can be heard up to one kilometre (0.6 miles) away. Leaping like this is called breaching. Lots of whales breach, but no one really knows why.

Why does a whale breach?

Some scientists think that the whale is shaking off itchy barnacles and lice from its skin. Some think that it is communicating with other whales. Or it might just be playing and having fun!

Orcas

Orcas are large, fierce water mammals. They are often called killer whales, even though they are actually dolphins! Orcas live in groups called pods, and they hunt in teams.

Breaching

Orcas can leap out of the water, jumping several metres above the surface. This might be a way of removing old skin or parasites.

Pectoral flippers act like paddles. The dolphin uses them to steer and stop.

A hunter's teeth

An orca's 40–50 sharp teeth grasp and tear its food. An orca doesn't chew – a small seal or sea lion can slide down its throat in one piece.

The dorsal fin keeps the dolphin from rolling over.

Find out more about orcas on the next page.

Orca babies

A mother orca usually has one baby every three to five years. A calf stays close to its mother to learn everything it needs to know.

Spy-hopping

By kicking its tail fluke, an orca can hold its head out of the water for several minutes and look around. It looks like a person treading water!

Orca hunt

Orcas work together as a team to catch their prey. They will surround a seal on an ice floe or chase a lone whale. It is difficult to escape an orca hunt.

Orca dinner

A lone Weddell seal doesn't stand a chance against a 4.5-tonne orca and its pod beneath the waves.

Superpod

There may be as many as 150 orcas in a single pod. Pod members "talk" to one another with clicks and whistles.

Tail slapping

By whacking the surface of the water with its tail, an orca can stun, or knock out, hundreds of fish at a time.

Food chain

Orcas are top predators of the sea.

Orca
The orca is a top predator, an animal that is never preyed on.

Seal
Seals are eaten by orcas, sharks, and whales. They eat fish and squid.

Squid
Using their long tentacles, squid catch small fish and krill to eat.

Krill
Near the bottom of the food chain, krill feast on teeny-tiny plants.

Each orca's fins are unique, just like fingerprints are unique to each human.

Catching a whale
A minke whale is faster than an orca, but it can't outswim a whole pod. The orcas chase, bite, and wear out the minke until it becomes dinner.

minke

Orcas' only enemies are humans, who may hunt them.

Whales and dolphins

These large – sometimes gigantic – mammals must breathe air at the ocean's surface. So they can't ever really sleep! Half of a whale's or dolphin's brain is awake at all times.

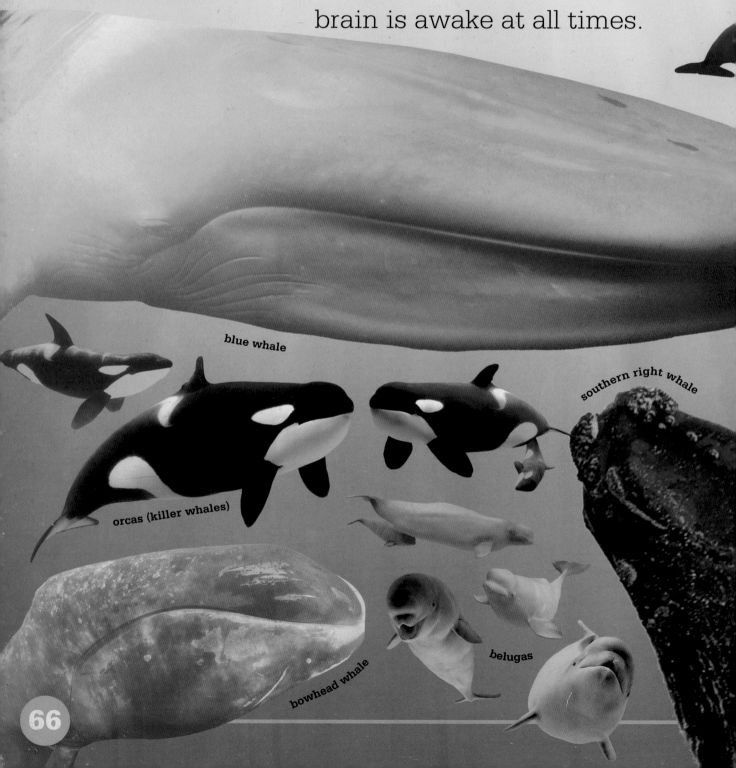

blue whale

southern right whale

orcas (killer whales)

bowhead whale

belugas

humpback whales

Antarctic minke whale

southern
bottlenose whale

fin whale

narwhals

hourglass dolphin

sperm whales

In the deep

The strangest of all animals lurk deep down in polar oceans. Temperatures are very cold. There are few predators. Creatures grow slowly but live for a long time, so some may be giants of their kinds.

ARCTIC OCEAN

Average depth: 1,205 metres (3,950 ft)
Lowest point: 5,567 metres (18,265 ft)

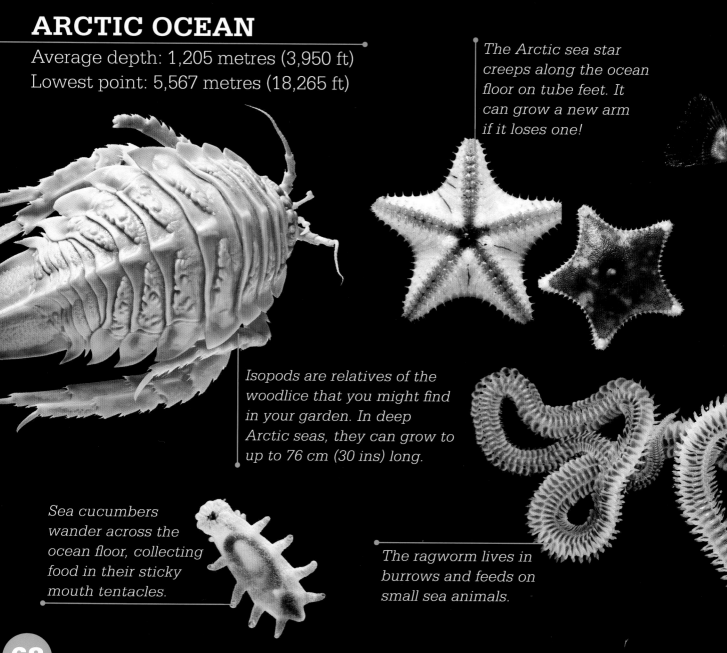

The Arctic sea star creeps along the ocean floor on tube feet. It can grow a new arm if it loses one!

Isopods are relatives of the woodlice that you might find in your garden. In deep Arctic seas, they can grow to up to 76 cm (30 ins) long.

Sea cucumbers wander across the ocean floor, collecting food in their sticky mouth tentacles.

The ragworm lives in burrows and feeds on small sea animals.

There are sponges in the Southern Ocean that are over

crabeater seal

SOUTHERN OCEAN

Average depth: 3,270 metres (10,730 ft)
Lowest point: 7,075 metres (23,210 ft)

The icefish's blood is transparent and acts like antifreeze. The fish can survive freezing waters 770 m (2,530 ft) deep.

The basket star's arms twist and coil around its prey. Tiny hooks keep the prey from escaping.

The plunderfish uses the whiskery barbel on its nose to search for food in dark waters.

barbel

1,000 years old!

In danger

Life at the poles is under threat. It's often humans who are causing the problems, even from far away.

Global warming

Car exhaust fumes and burning oil to make electricity produce a gas called carbon dioxide (CO_2). Too much CO_2 may be causing our planet to heat up. This means that less ice forms at the poles each winter.

All these human

Oil spills

Tankers carrying oil sometimes have big spills. One spill can kill many thousands of animals.

Without the sea ice, polar bears cannot catch enough seals to eat. The bears may go hungry.

Find out more about polar bears on pages 26–31.

fur seal

Krill live on the sea ice. Less ice means fewer krill. Many animals, such as fur seals, eat krill. They could be in danger if there isn't as much food.

WARNING

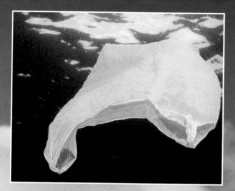

Litter
Rubbish left on beaches can drift all the way to polar seas. It can then harm the animals there.

Pollution
Factory fumes rise into the sky. The wind can blow them to the poles and pollute the ice.

Longline fishing
Chilly polar waters are home to many delicious fish. Seabirds diving for them can get tangled up in long fishing lines.

Boats can crash into whales. Also, noise from boat engines covers up the sounds that whales make to communicate with one another.

southern ....right whale

Albatross mistake floating rubbish for food and feed it to their chicks. The chicks choke and die.

What can you do?

We can all do things to help save the amazing wildlife at the poles. If everyone does just a little, we can make a great big difference.

········ **gentoo penguins**

Here are some ways you can help polar animals:

Switch it off!

Think about all the ways you can use less energy. Then you'll be producing less CO_2.

Clean up litter

Have fun at the beach, but remember to take all your rubbish home with you.

Check the label

If your family buys fish, check that it has been caught by hook and line rather than longline.

Weddell seal pup

Find out more

The more you learn about the poles, the more you will find out about how you can help.

Spread the word!

Tell your friends and family about the incredible animals at the poles. They'll want to save them, too! Explain what you are doing to help.

Interview with an

Name: Jaume Forcada
Profession: Sea mammal expert for the British Antarctic Survey

Q What do you do?

A I study marine animals in the Antarctic. I mostly research seals, whales, penguins, and albatross. At the moment, I'm finding out about fur seals.

Q Why are you interested in Antarctic animals?

A It's a pretty unexplored place, and I want to know how the animals live down there. I especially want to know if global warming is affecting them.

Q How often do you go to the Antarctic?

A I go every summer, which is from December to February in Antarctica. This is when the fur seal pups are born.

Q How do you get there?

A I fly from the UK to the Falkland Islands, just off the tip of South America. Then it takes 15 days to get to Bird Island, near Antarctica, in a ship called the *James Clark Ross*.

.... fur seal pup

Antarctic scientist

fur seal · · · · · ·

Q Do you camp on the ice?

A No. I stay at the research station with up to nine other scientists. It's warm and comfortable. I share a bedroom, eat in the lounge, and work in one of the labs.

Q What are you studying about fur seals?

A I'm studying the sizes of fur seal populations. I want to see if there are more seals than there were last year and other years, fewer, or the same number.

Q Where are the fur seal pups born?

A The seals breed on Bird Island every summer. I count the pups on one beach that is used as a study area. It is about the size of a tennis court.

Q How do you count the seals and their pups?

A The adults are marked with paint so they don't get counted more than once. The pups are given ID chips, just like the ones you might use to tag a pet cat or dog.

Q What have you learned?

A There are around one-third fewer seals born now than there were thirty years ago. We think this is because of global warming. Less sea ice means fewer krill, and that is what fur seals mostly eat.

Glossary

Antarctic
The area around the South Pole. The Antarctic includes the continent Antarctica and the waters that surround it. Most of Antarctica is covered in ice.

Antarctic Circle
An imaginary line on a map that circles the Antarctic.

Arctic
The area around the North Pole. Most of the Arctic is a frozen ocean. Its edges reach the tips of North America, Europe, and Asia.

Arctic Circle
An imaginary line on a map that circles the Arctic.

barnacle
A small sea creature that attaches itself to whales, rocks, and the bottoms of ships.

blubber
The layer of fat under the skin of a sea mammal that helps to keep it warm.

breach
To leap out of the water and into the air.

breathing hole
An opening in sea ice where seals can surface and breathe.

brood pouch
A flap of skin on a penguin, used to keep eggs and chicks warm.

camouflage
Natural colouring that helps animals blend in with their surroundings.

crèche
A group of penguin chicks gathered together for warmth and safety.

echolocation
A way that an animal can find food

and other objects in the dark or underwater. The animal makes sounds that bounce off the objects and echo back to the animal.

food chain
A series of living things that depend on one another for food. For example, grass is eaten by reindeer, which are then eaten by wolves.

ice floe
A large, flat sheet of floating ice, formed when sea ice breaks up in the spring.

krill
Tiny, shrimp-like sea creatures.

mammal
A warm-blooded animal that has hair and breathes air. Female mammals produce milk to feed their young.

migrate
To move from one place to another to find food, to have babies, or to escape from cold weather.

moult
To lose old feathers so that new ones can grow. Young birds moult as they become adults.

pod
A group of some sea mammals, such as whales, that swim and feed together.

polar
Near or having to do with the icy area around the North or South Pole.

predator
An animal that hunts other animals for food.

prey
An animal that is hunted by another animal as food.

sea ice
Frozen seawater.

streamlined
Shaped to slip easily through water or air.

tundra
Flat, treeless areas of the Arctic with permanently frozen soil.

Index

Thank you

Alamy Images: 67 cbr (Anthony Pierce), 39 bc (Arco Images/Wiede, U. & M.), 58 (blickwinkel/Maywald), 40 (blickwinkel/Peltomaeki), 13 b (david tipling), 10 bg, 11 bg (Fotofeeling/Westend61 GmbH), 64 b bg, 65 b bg (Francois Gohier/VWPics), 27 b, 80 (Heather Angel/Natural Visions), 36 b (Interfoto), 62 bg, 63 bg (Juniors Bildarchiv/F248), 1, 32 c fg, 33 c fg (Koji Kitagawa/SuperStock), 71 tr (Mark Dyball), 10 bc (Michael S. Nolan/age fotostock), 34, 35 (Photoshot), 41 main (Stefan Ernst/Picture Press), 13 t, 39 t, 39 c (Steven J. Kazlowski), 65 b (WaterFrame), 38 b (Wayne Lynch), 9 Arctic lemming (Wayne Lynch/All Canada Photos), 54 c bg, 55 c bg, 78, 79 (WorldFoto), 47 r (Zoonar GmbH); AP Images/Zoo Wuppertal: 29 ct; Corbis Images: 28 (Jenny E. Ross), 12 b bg, 13 b bg (Stefan Christmann); Dr. Jaume Forcada/British Antarctic Survey: 74 t; Dreamstime: 45 peregrine falcon (Brian Kushner), 44 ruddy turnstone (David Spates), 9 imperial shag, 45 bluethroat (Dmytro Pylypenko), 44 stonechat (Dule964), 44 Arctic skuas (Erectus), 44 whinchat (Florian Teodor Andronache), 44 sandhill crane (George Bailey), 44 Eurasian golden plover (Gerald Deboer), 44 greater white-fronted geese (Ginger Sanders), 8 polar bear, 9 polar bear (Glenn Nagel), 45 white-crowned sparrow (Glenn Price), 44 Swainson's thrush (Howard Cheek), back cover owl (Ianmaton), 8 Atlantic puffin (Isselee), 45 Baird's sandpiper (Janice Mccafferty), 9 king penguin chick (Jeremy Wee), 45 meadow pipit (Joan Egert), 67 ctl (Joanne Weston), 45 white-tailed eagle (Joshanon1), 33 ctfl (Lukas Blazek), 45 sanderling (Madd), back cover computer icon (Manaemedia), 44 semipalmated sandpiper, 44 snow goose, 45 green-winged teal (Michael Mill), 45 red-breasted merganser (Mikelane45), 9 wolverine, 33 ctfr (Mirage3), 45 horned lark (Mircea Costina), 9 musk ox calf (Naturablichter), 44 glaucous-winged gull (Pnwnature), 66 ct (Sergiy Mashchenko), 8 reindeer (Simone Winkler), 45 long-tailed duck (Steve Byland), 45 spotted sandpiper (Suebmtl), 45 northern pintail (Thomas Lozinski), 9 Canadian lynx kitten (Twildlife), cover seal, 8 harp seal pup (Vladimir Melnik), 8 emperor penguin, 55 t (Vladimir Seliverstov), 44 Arctic tern (Volkan Akgul), 44 red-throated diver, 45 semipalmated plover, 45 northern wheatear (Wkruck); Fotolia: 45 upland sandpiper (anotherlook), 17 bl penguins (axily), 66 cb (Christopher Meder), 43 t, 43 cr (drhfoto), 17 b bg (elnavegante), 16 polar bear (erectus), 54 br (Fabrice Beauchene), 16 bg sun (forplayday), 45 brambling (fotomaster), 48 bl (grondetphoto), 19 cl (hecke71), 16 penguin (javarman-), 48 cr (jbrandt), 19 c ice (Marius Graf), 70 t (Mikhail Perfilov), 48 tr (Nadezhda Bolotina), 17 Arctic fox (outdoorsman), 42 t (photo4emotion), 19 c icicles, 21 c icicles (Rumo), 67 ctr (Sebastian French), 20 b (Silver), 45 fox sparrow (Steve Byland), 51 bcr (Tatiana Volgutova), 18 c (visceralimage), 18 cr (Vladimir Melnik), 48 tl (withGod), 16 bg stars (Yuriy Mazur); Getty Images: 36 tc (Flip Nicklin/Minden Pictures), 22 tr inset, 56, 57 bg, 66 bfl (Paul Nicklen/National Geographic), 38 tl (Sue Flood), 9 wandering albatross (Visuals Unlimited, Inc./Joe McDonald), cover polar bears (Wayne R. Bilenduke); iStockphoto: 33 cbr (4kodiak), 2 bg, 3 bg (afhunta), 9 musk ox (Afonskaya), 66 br, 71 bl (Aifos), 23 cr inset (ailanlee), 49 br (Antagain), 12 t bg, 13 t bg (ArildHeitmann), 72 bc (Auke Holwerda), 70 bg, 71 bg (Avatar_023), cover bg, back cover bg (axily), 46 br (bjmc), 36 t bg, 37 t bg, 49 snowflakes, 68 t, 69 t bg (brainmaster), 43 br (ca2hill), 23 cl inset (cbarnesphotography), 43 bl (cliffwass), 54 bl, 70 cl (Coldimages), 66 bcl, 66 bcr (CostinT), 62 b (datmore), 70 bl (dawnn), 8 Arctic fox (DmitryND), 21 cl (dsischo), 29 cb (ekvals), 42 cr (ElementalImaging), 9 Adélie penguin (flammulated), 44 cliff swallow (Frank Leung), 19 c snow (Ganders), 16 bl inset (GentooMultimediaLimited), 2 b, 10 tr, 12 b, 18 cl, 27 tl, 73 bc (GlobalP), 76 bg, 77 bg (goinyk), 11 r (Grafissimo), 8 snow, 9 snow, 17 t bg, 26 br inset snow, 76 snow, 77 snow

(herpens), 71 br (hlansdown), 20 cl, 23 tl inset (HuntedDuck), 27 cbr (imagestock), 17 polar bear (JackF), 63 bl, 66 ctr (jandaly), 44 American pipit (jcrader), 57 br (JeffDSamuels71), 9 snowy owl (JensKlingebiel), 66 bg, 67 bg (jfybel), 26 bc, 29 b (JohnPitcher), 21 t penguins, 22 bc inset (jrphoto6), 46 bg, 47 bg (juhokuva), 17 b snow (Justin Horrocks), 29 c, 51 br, 57 tl (KeithSzafranski), 47 tl (kem528), 20 c (KingMatz1980), 20 t bg, 21 t bg (kkaplin), 42 t bg (Larissa Belova), 64 b, 65 cfl (Lazareva), 20 t penguin, 74 br, 75 b (lc66), 26 bl (LifesizeImages), 72 bl inset bg (LinnGreen), 21 c snow (loops7), 74 bl (Matt Naylor), 72 br (Matthew Dixon), 41 icicles (Merzavka), 4 inset (MichaelPrice), 8 ermine (mihailzhukov), 9 leopard seal (mike_matas), 44 black-throated diver, 46 t (MikeLane45), 4 t bg, 5 fg walrus, 5 b bg, 19 cr, 33 b (mikeuk), 9 chinstrap penguin (MOF), 10 bl (MogensTrolle), 22 br inset, 23 bl inset (MR1805), 42 cl (Ornitolog82), 65 t (oversnap), 70 br (pagadesign), 17 b Arctic tern (Pauline S Mills), 45 greater scaup (photofellow), 54 t bg, 55 t bg (plrphoto), 8 seal, 32 t (pum_eva), 73 bl (quavondo), cover penguin (RichLindie), 42 c bg, 43 c bg (roc8jas), 66 ctl (Rpsycho), 10 tl (RyersonClark), 19 b (samsem67), 71 tc (savas keskiner), 63 br (sethakan), 67 br (ShaneGross), 27 ctfr (shuchunke), 43 cl (sjulienphoto), 49 snowflakes (Spauln), 30, 31 (SylvieBouchard), 27 plates (t_kimura), 59 t (temis), 17 br penguin, 73 br (thp73), 70 cr (USO), 27 tr (VisualCommunications), 49 snowflakes (Vitalina Rybakova), 17 t Arctic tern (zakshaw), 12 t, 32 cl, 33 t (zanskar); Nature Picture Library/Fred Olivier: 55 bl; Planetary Visions Ltd.: 17 t globe, 19 globes, 21 globes; Robert Pitman: 64 t; Scholastic, Inc.: 59 b; Science Source: 33 cbl (Alexander Semenov), 21 cr (ANT Photo Library), 8 Arctic hare, 37 tr (Art Wolfe), 11 l, 65 cr, 69 cl, 69 br, 69 cr (British Antarctic Survey), 27 cbc, 32 bl, 48 br, 49 tl, 50 t, 50 bc, 51 t, 51 bl, 51 bcl, 57 bl (Bryan and Cherry Alexander), 67 cbl, 67 bc (Christian Darkin), 42 b (Christopher Swann), 8 black guillemot (Dr. P. Marazzi), 33 ctr (G. Carleton Ray), 47 bl (George Holton), 22 bl inset (Gregory G. Dimijian, M.D.), 18 b (Ignacio Yufera/FLPA), 18 t, 19 t bg (John Devries), 9 cape petrel, 45 long-tailed skua (John Shaw), 17 b globe (M-Sat Ltd), 45 American tree sparrow (Manuel Presti), 68 cl (Natural History Museum, London), 49 cl (Ron Sanford); Seapics.com: 66 t, 67 ctc; Shutterstock, Inc.: 20 b inset (3drenderings), 3 t, 9 south polar skua (AndreAnita), 27 ctfl, 36 tl, 67 bl (Andreas Meyer), 59 ct, 65 cfr (aquapix), 49 bl (bikeriderlondon), 65 krill (bluehand), 9 little auk, 21 b, 45 long-tailed skua, 55 br (BMJ), 16 globe, 43 globe (Bruce Rolff), 20 cr, 52, 53 (Dmytro Pylypenko), 5 b, 29 t, 39 bl, 39 br, 76 fg, 77 fg (Eric Isselee), 45 Lapland bunting (Erni), 37 cr (Evlakhov Valeriy), 44 pomarine skua (feathercollector), 33 ctc, 57 tr, 57 c (Gentoo Multimedia Limited), 45 common redpoll (Gerry Alvarez-Murphy), 22 frames, 23 frames, 50 bl (Iakov Filimonov), 27 ctr (Incredible Arctic), 37 b (Ivan Histand), 59 c (Jay Ondreicka), 26 br inset seal (Joe Stone), 59 cb (John Tunney), 22 tl inset, 67 tl (Joost van Uffelen), 9 snow petrel (jurra8), 46 bl (LittleMiss), 36 tr, 37 cl, 66 bc (Luna Vandoorne), 50 br (Marcel Jancovic), 65 cl, 69 t (Mariusz Potocki), 45 tundra swans (MCarter), cover killer whale (Mike Price), 75 t (Moritz Buchty), 24, 25, 60, 61 (NancyS), 22 bg, 23 bg (nikolae), 33 ctl (Peter Zijlstra), 72 bl inset (Rasulov), 67 cbr (Shane Gross), 68 bl, 68 cr, 68 br, 69 bl (Solodov Alexey), 8 least weasel (Stephan Morris), 10 br (Stephen Lavery), 38 bg, 39 bg (Tom Middleton), 26 t (VikOl), 27 ctl, 27 cbl (Vladimir Melnik), 2 t, 6, 7, 14, 15, 72 t, 73 t, 73 t bg (Volodymyr Goinyk), 26 bg, 27 bg, 32 c bg, 33 c bg (White Rabbit83); Superstock, Inc./NHPA: 67 tr; Thinkstock: 71 tl (MikaelEriksson), 45 rough-legged buzzard (RCKeller); Wikipedia: 54 bc (Didier Descouens/Museum of Toulouse), 23 br inset (Tasteofcrayons), 23 tr inset (Wooley Booley/Mike Beauregard).